CHRISTIAN DATING:
THE Q & A BOOK

250 DATING QUESTIONS – 250 BIBLE-BASED ANSWERS

♥ ♥ ♥

RITA HENDERSON

WESTBOW®
PRESS
A DIVISION OF THOMAS NELSON
& ZONDERVAN

WestBow Press books may be ordered through booksellers or by contacting:

WestBow Press
A Division of Thomas Nelson & Zondervan
1663 Liberty Drive
Bloomington, IN 47403
www.westbowpress.com
1 (866) 928-1240

ISBN: 978-1-4908-1885-6 (sc)
ISBN: 978-1-4908-1886-3 (hc)
ISBN: 978-1-4908-1884-9 (e)

Library of Congress Control Number: 2013922121

Print information available on the last page.

WestBow Press rev. date: 03/24/2018

In memory of Alma Jenkins (mom)

Special thanks to those who assisted me:
Cynthia B. Sherrill
Lysa Jenkins
Bernice Brooks-Harvey
Marjorie Clay
Patricia Franklin

Special thanks to those who inspired me:
Christian Mathews
Megan Turner
Serenity Francisco
Jennifer J. Henderson
Myeisha McKay
Kenneth Gildersleeve Jr.
Tonya Rutledge
James Edward Henderson III
Gina Houser

Special thanks to those who motivated me:
Michael Henderson
Jan Gildersleeve
Claudius Jenkins

I pray that your love will overflow more and more, and that you will keep on growing in knowledge and understanding.

Philippians 1:9 NLT

Bible Versions Used:

ERV – Easy-to-Read Version

ESV – English Standard Version

KJV – King James Version

NASB – New American Standard Bible

NCV – New Century Version

NIRV – New International Reader's Version

NIV – New International Version

NKJV – New King James Version

NLT – New Living Translation

The Message – The Message

TNIV – Today's New International Version

Contents

....

Chapter 3 – Christian Behavior

Should Christians date nonbelievers?

How should Christians behave in relationships?

How can I glorify God in a Christian relationship?

How should I elevate God in a Christian relationship?

How beneficial is a pure heart in a Christian relationship?

Is prideful behavior ever a virtue in Christian relationships?

How can I focus on a Christ-centered life while in a relationship?

Should we admit our faults in Christian relationships?

How can gossip influence a relationship?

How essential is it to account for our actions in a relationship?

How important is humility in a relationship?

How can I discern the contents of my partner's heart?

Can my thinking determine my destiny in a relationship?

Why are give-and-take relationships healthier?

Why shouldn't possessions define Christians in a relationship?

How important are people skills in a Christian relationship?

Why is being selfless so significant in a relationship?

Why should we provide a shoulder to cry on for our mate?

Is it wrong to judge my partner in a relationship?

Why is conceited behavior frowned upon in Christian relationships?

What are the benefits of a spiritually fit life?

Chapter 9 – Fear

Chapter 10 – Forgiveness

Chapter 11 – Guidance

Chapter 14 – Joy

Are there ways to know if my partner is happy?

How should I embrace the positive moments in a relationship?

What are the advantages of a happy heart in a relationship?

Why should we motivate each other in a relationship?

How can I maintain a joyous spirit while dating?

Chapter 15 – Kindness

Should we give generously to each other in a Christian relationship?

Why should my partner and I always respond with a positive attitude toward each other?

Why is a kind heart an asset in a Christian relationship?

What is the most attractive trait in a Christian man?

How beneficial is a tender greeting extended to my partner?

Why is expressing compassion towards others essential?

How should Christians treat an ungrateful partner?

How does God want us to behave toward each other?

Why should we give to each other freely and cheerfully?

How should a Christian woman communicate?

Why is timing so significant when communicating?

What are the benefits of always doing right towards one another?

Chapter 16 – Love

How should I express my love to my partner?

How will I know if my partner is disobedient to God?

What if my partner does not obey all of God's rules?

What is sound advice for Christian relationships?

Why should I watch my words when communicating with my partner?

Prior to marriage, how should I spend my single years?

How can I enhance my spiritual growth?

I am a faithful Christian, so why am I still single?

How do I respond to those opposing my obedience to God's word?

Chapter 18 – Pain

Will God help the brokenhearted heal?

Why is there sadness in relationships?

How do I handle rejection in a relationship?

Is a bitter heart capable of loving others?

Why are Christians discouraged against seeking revenge when betrayed in a relationship?

How do I overcome my hurt feelings in a relationship?

Chapter 19 – Patience

How can I avoid becoming too anxious for a relationship?

How can I avoid becoming frustrated waiting for the right mate?

Has God forgotten about my desire to marry?

How critical is patience in a Christian relationship?

Why should I continue to wait for love?

Will patience help to eliminate some of the problems in a relationship?

Why is tolerance for each other beneficial in a relationship?

How should I nurture a healthy relationship?

Why should I avoid being overly sensitive while communicating?

Chapter 20 – Peace

How can I experience a harmonious relationship?

How can I avoid becoming anxious about falling in love?

Why is keeping the peace critical in a Christian relationship?

Why should I remain positive when feeling negative in a relationship?

What are the benefits of being a peacemaker in a relationship?

How important is my happiness in a Christian relationship?

How can we empower each other in a Christian relationship?

What is the function of a peacemaker in a relationship?

Chapter 21 – Prayer

Should I pray for a Christian husband?

Should we pray together for a blessed relationship?

Why is daily prayer significant in Christian relationships?

Will God answer my prayers for a godly husband?

Why is it important to continue to give thanks during trying times in a relationship?

....

Chapter 26 – Worry

How can I stop obsessing about finding a Christian mate?

Why is worrying considered a waste of time?

How can I be supportive when my partner is consumed with worry?

How should I manage anxiety in a relationship?

Where can I turn when my relationship concerns are stressing me out?

10 Desirable Traits of a Christian Mate

1. Devout Christian: *2 Corinthians 6:14 (NIV)* ☐
   Do not be yoked together with unbelievers. For what do righteousness and wickedness have in common? Or what fellowship can light have with darkness?

2. Good Tempered: *Proverbs 22:24 (NCV)* ☐
   Don't make friends with quick-tempered people or spend time with those who have bad tempers. If you do, you will be like them. Then you will be in real danger.

3. Christian Character: *1 Corinthians 15:33 (NIRV)* ☐
   Don't let anyone fool you. Bad companions make a good person bad.

4. Obedient to God: *2 Timothy 3:5 (ERV)* ☐
   They will go on pretending to be devoted to God, but they will refuse to let that "devotion" change the way they live. Stay away from these people!

5. Respectful: *Hebrews 11:6 (NLV)* ☐
   Show respect to all men. Love the Christians. Honor God with love and fear. Respect the head leader of the country.

6. Forgiving: *Mark 11:25–26 (ERV)* ☐
   When you are praying and you remember that you are angry with another person about something, forgive that person. Forgive them so that your Father in heaven will also forgive your sins.

7. Honesty: *Proverbs 26:28 (NIRV)* ☐
   A tongue that tells lies hates the people it hurts. And words that seem to praise you destroy you.

8. Kindness: *Proverbs 19:22 NASB* ☐
   What is desirable in a man is his kindness. And it is better to be a poor man than a liar.

9. Communicator: *Colossians 4:6 (The Message)* ☐
   Be gracious in your speech. The goal is to bring out the best in others in a conversation, not put them down, not cut them out.

10. Patience: *Revelation 14:12 (NIRV)* ☐
    God's people need to be very patient. They are the ones who obey God's commands. They remain faithful to Jesus.

....

Introduction

Many books focus on secular dating relationships. However, very few explore the topic of Christian dating. Regrettably, a great number of single Christians are seeking definitive answers to their complex relationship questions, from a biblical perspective. *Christian Dating: The Q & A Book* provides the sought-after answers to these important questions.

While I am aware the Bible does not directly address the subject of dating; I recognize, as a Christian, the Holy Bible is the instruction book on how God wants us to conduct ourselves. I acknowledge the goal in studying the Bible is to understand God's word, and most important, apply the godly principles of the Bible to our daily living. This is how we honor God!

Why am I confident the Bible provides the scriptural answers to our everyday concerns? The "Sufficiency of Scripture" is a significant doctrine, which confirms God's word is sufficient and proves we need not seek instruction elsewhere to discern God's will!

Paul the Apostle stresses the very same concept to Timothy in 2 Timothy 3:16–17 (ERV):

All Scripture is given by God. And all Scripture is useful for teaching and for showing people what is wrong in their lives. It is useful for correcting faults and teaching the right way to live. By using the Scriptures, those who serve God will be prepared and will have everything they need to do every good work.

Christian Dating: The Q & A Book shares with you the application of God's word to over 250 relationship questions. You will gain essential dating advice, such as how to handle your emotions, fears, heartbreak and worries. Fundamental Christian knowledge is provided on discernment, inner beauty, love, patience, respect, sexual purity and trust. My goal is to help Christian singles seeking biblical guidance in their dating relationships.

CHAPTER 1

Anger

Christians should make a conscious effort to control circumstances that alter their moods for the worse. This chapter demonstrates how to respond when faced with adverse conditions, which test our tolerance and self-control. The biblical responses presented reinforce Christian values, such as managing anger, controlling your temper, not repaying evil for evil, and knowing when to hold your tongue. In summary, the chapter demonstrates how an anger-management problem can severely damage a loving Christian relationship and how the principles within Scripture can rescue it.

♥   ♥   ♥

How should I respond to verbal attacks in a relationship?

Apply Bible principles from *1 Peter 3:9 NLT*

Don't repay evil for evil. Don't retaliate with insults when people insult you. Instead, pay them back with a blessing. That is what God has called you to do, and he will bless you for it.

Verbal abuse can take shape in many forms, such as ridicule, humiliation, manipulation, embarrassment, and the "silent treatment." It can make the recipient feel unappreciated, misunderstood, and unsupported. Remember, partners respect each other in healthy Christian relationships.

Is it wrong to hold grudges against each other?

Apply Bible principles from *Leviticus 19:18 (The Message)*

Don't seek revenge or carry a grudge against any of your people. Love your neighbor as yourself. I am God.

Holding a grudge is unhealthy for us. In fact, research shows that holding on to past offenses can bring on depression in both men and women alike.

Why is it helpful to watch my temper while communicating?

Apply Bible principles from *Ecclesiastes 7:9 NLT*

Control your temper, for anger labels you a fool.

It is also wise to be mindful of your non-verbal communication, such as facial expressions, rolling of eyes, arm-crossing, sarcastic gestures, and tone of voice.

Is there a response I should avoid when my partner is upset?

Apply Bible principles from *Psalms 37:8 ERV*

Don't become so angry and upset that you, too, want to do evil.

Many times when we are upset, we react rather than respond. When someone is reacting, he or she is often in "attack mode" and is perceived in a negative light. However, in response mode, the person is very calm and composed and is perceived in a positive light.

Why are poor attitudes unhealthy for dating relationships?

Apply Bible principles from *Proverbs 3:31 The Message*

Don't walk around with a chip on your shoulder, always spoiling for a fight. Don't try to be like those who shoulder their way through life. Why be a bully? "Why not?" you say. Because God can't stand twisted souls. It's the straightforward who get his respect.

Bullies feel unworthy and use their tactics to get attention. Remember, secure people who act confidently will not become victims.

Why should Christians avoid partners with an anger problem?

Apply Bible principles from *Proverbs 22:24 NCV*

Don't make friends with quick-tempered people or spend time with those who have bad tempers. If you do, you will be like them. Then you will be in real danger.

There is a distinction between aggressive and assertive behavior. Angry behavior (aggressive) is used to intimidate and abuse the other party. However, an assertive person usually stands up for himself or herself, or what he or she believes in, but not in a confrontational manner.

How should an intelligent Christian manage anger in a relationship?

Apply Bible principles from *Proverbs 19:11 The Message*

Smart people know how to hold their tongue; their grandeur is to forgive and forget.

Many of us try to excuse our angry episodes by blaming others for our actions. However, anger is an internal problem that results in external outbursts. Keep in mind, becoming angry is not a sin, but acting on the anger is sinful. The solution is to take the problem to God.

Why are verbal outbursts damaging to a Christian relationship?

Apply Bible principles from *Proverbs 30:33 NCV*

Just as stirring milk makes butter, and twisting noses makes them bleed, so stirring up anger causes trouble.

You have the power to control how you respond to tough situations! Therefore, be mindful that you do not allow the actions of others control your emotions. Pray during these difficult times and ask God to help you.

Why should Christians control their rage during disputes?

Apply Bible principles from *James 1:20 ERV*

Anger does not help you live the way God wants.

Try to minimize your emotions when discussing important issues and significant decisions. Remember, Christians should exemplify Christ-like behavior at all times.

How critical is self-control in a relationship?

Apply Bible principles from *Proverbs 25:28 The Message*

A person without self-control is like a house with its doors and windows knocked out.

According to the principles of Scripture, Christians must exercise self-control to make the right choices in their lives.

CHAPTER 2

Character

♥ ♥ ♥

There is more than one definition of the word character. To simplify matters, we will define it as "our internal values that determine our external actions." Good character is an asset that encompasses one's integrity, moral strength, and principles. It speaks to one's inner spirit and informs who the person is, even when no one is looking. According to Evangelist Billy Graham, *"When wealth is lost, nothing is lost; when health is lost, something is lost; when character is lost, all is lost."* This chapter highlights the value of Christian character in a dating relationship.

What character traits should a Christian mate have?

Apply Bible principles from *Proverbs 6:16–19 The Message*

Here are six things God hates, and one more that he loathes with a passion: eyes that are arrogant, a tongue that lies, hands that murder the innocent, a heart that hatches evil plots, feet that race down a wicked track, a mouth that lies under oath, a troublemaker in the family.

If we are followers of Christ, our character and conduct should reflect Him. As Christians, if the Holy Spirit is operating inside, evidence of this should be witnessed on the outside, through our actions and deeds.

Why should Christians avoid partners who love money?

Apply Bible principles from *Matthew 6:24–25 NIV*

No one can serve two masters, for either he will hate the one and love the other, or he will be devoted to the one and despise the other. You cannot serve God and money.

Many Christians believe that money is evil, but the truth is, the love of money is evil. Remember, Christians should not allow idols to come between God and us.

Why should girls of good character avoid bad boys?

Apply Bible principles from *1 Corinthians 15:33 NIRV*

Don't let anyone fool you. Bad companions make a good person bad.

Insecure people, both men and women alike, are usually the victims of manipulation. However, if the spirit of God dwells within us, we know who we are in Christ, and it will become difficult for anyone to manipulate our thinking or actions.

Why does alcohol addiction negatively impact a Christian relationship?

Apply Bible principles from *Proverbs 20:1 NLV*

Wine makes people act in a foolish way. Strong drink starts fights. Whoever is fooled by it is not wise.

We are aware that drinking alcohol in excess is known to impair one's thinking. Of course, this can lead to poor communication and unwarranted arguments within the relationship. Furthermore, scientific research has linked over consumption of alcohol to aggression and domestic violence.

Who should single Christians avoid when choosing a mate?

Apply Bible principles from *2 Timothy 3:17 ESV*

But understand this, that in the last days there will come times of difficulty. For people will be lovers of self, lovers of money, proud, arrogant, abusive, disobedient to their parents, ungrateful, unholy, heartless, unappeasable, slanderous, without self-control, brutal, not loving good, treacherous, reckless, swollen with conceit, lovers of pleasure rather than lovers of God, having the appearance of godliness, but denying its power. Avoid such people.

When seeking a life-mate, Christians should look for devout partners who also want to lead a life that is "holy and pleasing to God." This behavior should reflect the Christian beliefs observed in the Bible.

Why is generosity encouraged in Christian relationships?

Apply Bible principles from *Proverbs 11:25 NIV*

A generous person will prosper; whoever refreshes others will be refreshed.

If we keep our hand closed, we will never lose anything; however, we will not gain anything either! Again, Bible Scripture advises us, "God loves a cheerful giver."

Can bad habits harm a Christian relationship?

Apply Bible principles from *Proverbs 26:11 NIRV*

A foolish person who does the same foolish things again is like a dog that returns to where it has thrown up.

Proverbs 26:11 NIRV

This passage of Scripture reminds me of the definition of insanity—doing the same thing over and over and expecting a different result. In our dating relationships, we should make a conscious effort to learn from our past mistakes and move on.

What are the challenges when dating a materialistic person?

Apply Bible principles from *Ecclesiastes 5:10 ERV*

Those who love money will never be satisfied with the money they have. Those who love wealth will not be satisfied when they get more and more. This is also senseless.

As a Christian, we cannot allow material items (idols) to come between God and us. So a wise choice is a mate who shares common Christian values.

Why are we encouraged to date financially responsible Christians?

Apply Bible principles from *Romans 13:5–7 The Message*

That's why you must live responsibly—not just to avoid punishment but also because it's the right way to live. That's also why you pay taxes—so that an orderly way of life can be maintained. Fulfill your obligations as a citizen. Pay your taxes, pay your bills, respect your leaders.

Everything we own belongs to God. Therefore, when it comes to financial responsibility, we should depend on his guidance and direction. To ensure obedience, as Christians, we must be disciplined and dedicated. Our partners should be similarly committed.

Why are arrogant people poor relationship choices?

Apply Bible principles from *Proverbs 11:2 The Message*

The stuck-up fall flat on their faces, but down-to-earth people stand firm.

Arrogance is a weakness! The dictionary defines arrogance as an offensive display of superiority or self-importance and overbearing pride. Unfortunately, prideful people rarely admit fault. In a Christian relationship, we should be humble and think of others as better than ourselves; thus allowing open communication.

CHAPTER 3

Christian Behavior

The trademarks of Christian behavior consist of love, joy, peace, patience, kindness, goodness, faithfulness, gentleness, and self-control. Our actions please God when we adhere to these characteristics. Furthermore, if we want a committed Christian relationship, it will be less complicated to travel this path with another Christian devoted to being a doer of the Word. However, we must beware of a person who calls himself or herself a believer, yet does not exhibit god-like behavior. In this case, we proceed with caution remembering Matthew 10:16 *"be wise as serpents yet harmless as doves."* Keep in mind, our Christian beliefs do not make us a noble person; however, our behavior does! This chapter stresses the importance of Christian behavior in a devoted Christian relationship.

♥ ♥ ♥

Should Christians date nonbelievers?

Apply Bible principles from *2 Corinthians 6:14 NIV*

Do not be yoked together with unbelievers. For what do righteousness and wickedness have in common? Or what fellowship can light have with darkness?

The principles of Christian dating are quite different from those of the secular world. Therefore, choose a partner who is committed to the same Christian values and beliefs as you.

How should Christians behave in relationships?

Apply Bible principles from *Romans 12:21 NLV*

Do not let sin have power over you. Let good have power over sin!

If you stay connected to the Word daily, it will support your efforts in avoiding the many worldly temptations.

How can I glorify God in a Christian relationship?

Apply Bible principles from *Matthew 5:16 ERV*

In the same way, you should be a light for other people. Live so that they will see the good things you do and praise your Father in heaven.

The best way to glorify God in your relationship is to honor him and set an exemplary model for other Christians.

How should I elevate God in a Christian relationship?

Apply Bible principles from *John 3:30 KJV*

He (Jesus Christ) must increase, but I must decrease.

God has given us the gift of life, and leading a virtuous life is our gift back to Him.

How beneficial is a pure heart in a Christian relationship?

Apply Bible principles from *Matthew 5:8 The Message*

You're blessed when you get your inside world—your mind and heart— put right. Then you can see God in the outside world.

Possessing a clean heart indicates that God's concerns are a priority in your life.

Is prideful behavior ever a virtue in Christian relationships?

Apply Bible principles from *Proverbs 29:23 ERV*

Your pride can bring you down. Humility will bring you honor.

You must release the pride to receive God's goodness.

How can I focus on a Christ-centered life while in a relationship?

Apply Bible principles from *Exodus 23:2 ERV*

Don't do something just because everyone else is doing it. If you see a group of people doing wrong, don't join them. You must not let them persuade you to do wrong things—you must do what is right and fair.

When we keep God's commandments, it motivates us to lead a life that honors God.

Should we admit to our faults in a Christian relationship?

Apply Bible principles from *Proverbs 28:13 ERV*

Whoever hides their sins will not be successful, but whoever confesses their sins and stops doing wrong will receive mercy.

When Christians admit fault when they're wrong, it shows spiritual maturity as well as humility.

How can gossip influence a relationship?

Apply Bible principles from *Proverbs 26:20 ERV*

Without wood, a fire goes out. Without gossip, arguments stop.

A person suffering from low self-esteem is usually the person to spread gossip. A Christian should not tear others down with scandalous chatter. It would be a more productive use of his or her time to ask God for help regarding his or her own feelings of insignificance.

How essential is it to account for our actions in a relationship?

Apply Bible principles from *2 Corinthians 5:10 NLV*

For all of us must stand before Christ when He says who is guilty or not guilty. Each one will receive pay for what he has done. He will be paid for the good or the bad done while he lived in this body.

Christians must take responsibility for their actions according to the governing principles presented in the Bible.

How important is humility in a relationship?

Apply Bible principles from *Matthew 5:5 NCV*

They are blessed who are humble, for the whole earth will be theirs.

In regard to humility, I am stressing a humble spirit versus humble behavior. A person can exhibit humble behavior and not possess a humble spirit. However, if one has a humble spirit, he or she can only demonstrate humble behavior.

How can I discern the contents of my partner's heart?

Apply Bible principles from *Matthew 12:33–37 ERV*

If you want good fruit, you must make the tree good. If your tree is not good, it will have bad fruit. A tree is known by the kind of fruit it produces. You snakes! You are so evil. How can you say anything good? What people say with their mouths comes from what fills their hearts. Those who are good have good things saved in their hearts. That's why they say good things. But those who are evil have hearts full of evil, and that's why they say things that are evil. I tell you that everyone will have to answer for all the careless things they have said. This will happen on the Day of Judgment. Your words will be used to judge you. What you have said will show whether you are right or whether you are guilty."

The mouth reveals what the heart conceals.

Can my thinking determine my destiny in a relationship?

Apply Bible principles from *Romans 12:2 NLT*

Don't copy the behavior and customs of this world, but let God transform you into a new person by changing the way you think. Then you will learn to know God's will for you, which is good and pleasing and perfect.

If you are thinking godly thoughts, you will exhibit godly behavior, and follow His plan designed especially for you.

Why are give-and-take relationships healthier?

Apply Bible principles from *Proverbs 11:24–25 The Message*

The world of the generous gets larger and larger; the world of the stingy gets smaller and smaller.

The one who blesses others is abundantly blessed; those who help others are helped.

Giving to others brings blessings to the giver.

Why shouldn't possessions define Christians in a relationship?

Apply Bible principles from *Luke 12:15 The Message*

Speaking to the people, he went on, "Take care! Protect yourself against the least bit of greed. Life is not defined by what you have, even when you have a lot."

The heart of a Christian cannot be defined by worldly possessions.

How important are people skills in a Christian relationship?

Apply Bible principles from *Proverbs 18:1 NIV*

An unfriendly person pursues selfish ends and against all sound judgment starts quarrels.

Always respond in loving kindness without displaying any signs of aggression or hostility toward your partner.

Why is being selfless so significant in a relationship?

Apply Bible principles from *Philippians 2:4 NKJV*

Let each of you look out not only for his own interests, but also for the interests of others.

As Christians, being selfless involves doing for each other without looking for personal gain.

Why should we provide a shoulder to cry on for our mate?

Apply Bible principles from *Galatians 6:2 ESV*

Help each other with your troubles. When you do this, you are obeying the law of Christ.

Compassion is not to be confused with pity. Compassion is reaching out to understand the suffering of others, not merely feeling sorry for them.

Is it wrong to judge my partner in a relationship?

Apply Bible principles from *Matthew 7:1–5 NLV*

Do not say what is wrong in other people's lives. Then other people will not say what is wrong in your life. You will be guilty of the same things you find in others. When you say what is wrong in others, your words will be used to say what is wrong in you. Why do you look at the small piece of wood in your brother's eye, and do not see the big piece of wood in your own eye? How can you say to your brother, 'Let me take that small piece of wood out of your eye,' when there is a big piece of wood in your own eye? You who pretend to be someone you are not, first take the big piece of wood out of your own eye. Then you can see better to take the small piece of wood out of your brother's eye.

It is very difficult to maintain a loving, caring and nurturing relationship if you are standing in judgment of each other.

Why is conceited behavior frowned upon in Christian relationships?

Apply Bible principles from *Proverbs 27:2 NCV*

Don't praise yourself. Let someone else do it. Let the praise come from a stranger and not from your own mouth.

Let someone else sing your praises. Remember, God loves a humble spirit.

What are the benefits of a spiritually fit life?

Apply Bible principles from *1 Timothy 4:8 The Message*

Exercise daily in God—no spiritual flabbiness, please! Workouts in the gymnasium are useful, but a disciplined life in God is far more so, making you fit both today and forever. You can count on this. Take it to heart.

No one can deny that physical fitness is beneficial to your health. However, being spiritually fit benefits all aspects of your life.

♥ ♥ ♥

CHAPTER 4

Communication

Communication is the key to success in relationships. Therefore, we must grasp the two vital ingredients to communicating, such as speaking and listening. When speaking we should organize our thoughts before sharing them with our partner. This will help us to keep focus on the subject matter. However, to receive a message effectively, we must engage in active listening. Which requires us to repeat to our partner what we heard. Keep in mind that the highest level of respect you can show your partner is by listening to what he or she has to say. In this chapter, I stress the value of communication within a Christian relationship with topics such as, how to avoid arguments, speak to each other with respect, become an excellent listener, and accept constructive criticism.

♥ ♥ ♥

How problematic is nagging for men?

Apply Bible principles from *Proverbs 21:9 NLT*

It's better to live alone in the corner of an attic than with a quarrelsome wife in a lovely home.

Nagging is persistent faultfinding, complaints, or demands. If problems arise, learn to discuss them respectfully, in a pleasant tone, always showing compassion for the listener.

How important is listening to my partner in a relationship?

Apply Bible principles from *Proverbs 25:28 NLT*

Spouting off before listening to the facts is both shameful and foolish.

Listening is critical in any relationship. Therefore, when communicating with one another, always be present in mind and body.

How can my partner and I communicate successfully?

Apply Bible principles from *Proverbs 29:20 ESV*

...Let every person be quick to hear, slow to speak, slow to anger.

Always make eye contact with your partner when communicating, as well as staying alert. This shows respect to the other person and confirms that you have a genuine interest in what he or she has to say.

How can I communicate better with my partner in a relationship?

Apply Bible principles from *Proverbs 15:1 ESV*

A soft answer turns away wrath, but a harsh word stirs up anger.

It is also smart to pay attention to your tone of voice when speaking. Remember, it is not always what you say but how you say it. Furthermore, avoid any internal and external distractions while you are communicating..

Can we avoid the back and forth bickering in a relationship?

Apply Bible principles from *Philippians 2:14 NIRV*

Do everything without finding fault or arguing. Then you will be pure and without blame.

Always maintain a positive attitude when conversing, even if the subject matter is difficult. Don't compete to be right, instead strive to be fair within the relationship.

Why is profanity discouraged in Christian relationships?

Apply Bible principles from *James 3:10 ESV*

From the same mouth come blessing and cursing. My brothers, these things ought not to be so.

"Profanity makes ignorance audible." – Author unknown

Why is effective communication so important in a relationship?

Apply Bible principles from *Colossians 4:6 The Message*

Be gracious in your speech. The goal is to bring out the best in others in a conversation, not put them down, not cut them out.

Communicating conveys to our partner what we are thinking and vice-versa. It is the best vehicle to bond with one another.

How can I become a great listener of my partner in a relationship?

Apply Bible principles from *Proverbs 18:13 ERV*

Let people finish speaking before you try to answer them. That way you will not embarrass yourself and look foolish.

Allowing your partner to complete his or her thoughts without interruption is a common courtesy. Likewise, make sure you are listening to understand and not just listening to give a reply.

Why should I learn to accept constructive criticism from my partner?

Apply Bible principles from *Proverbs 27:5–6 ERV*

Open criticism is better than hidden love. You can trust what your friend says, even when it hurts. But your enemies want to hurt you, even when they act nice.

Be watchful of your emotions when it comes to dealing with constructive criticism from others; especially those closest to you.

Why should I think before speaking to my partner?

Apply Bible principles from *Proverbs 12:18 ERV*

Speak without thinking, and your words can cut like a knife. Be wise and your words can heal.

We should think before speaking because our emotions can take over our thought process. When this happens, we may say things we will later regret.

How important is my choice of words when communicating?

Apply Bible principles from *Proverbs 18:21 The Message*

Words kill, words give life; they're either poison or fruit—you choose.

During a conversation, our choice of words is important, as well as our tone of voice and body language.

How can my partner and I agree to disagree successfully?

Apply Bible principles from *James 1:19 The Message*

Post this at all the intersections, dear friends: Lead with your ears, follow up with your tongue, and let anger straggle along in the rear. God's righteousness doesn't grow from human anger. So throw all spoiled virtue and cancerous evil in the garbage. In simple humility, let our gardener, God, landscape you with the Word, making a salvation-garden of your life.

In a relationship, we may not always agree, but we should always acknowledge each other's point of view.

Why does consistent arguing between partners destroy relationships?

Apply Bible principles from *Proverbs 17:1 NLV*

A dry piece of food with peace and quiet is better than a house full of food with fighting.

Constant arguing can be harmful to our health as well as the health of the relationship.

Can my words encourage my partner?

Apply Bible principles from *Ephesians 4:29 The Message*

When you talk, don't say anything bad. But say the good things that people need—whatever will help them grow stronger. Then what you say will be a blessing to those who hear you.

Speaking encouraging words to our partner is very soothing. This gives our partner hope for the future of the relationship.

How can I minimize the negativity in our conversations?

Apply Bible principles from *1 Peter 3:10 ERV*

The Scriptures say, "If you want to enjoy true life and have only good days, then avoid saying anything hurtful, and never let a lie come out of your mouth."

Your positive thoughts will lead to positive words and actions.

How can I prevent confusion from leading to chaos in a relationship?

Apply Bible principles from *1 Peter 3:8–11 ESV*

Finally, all of you have unity of mind, sympathy, brotherly love, a tender heart, and a humble mind. Do not repay evil for evil or reviling for reviling, but on the contrary, bless, for to this you were called, that you may obtain a blessing. For "Whoever desires to love life and see good days, let him keep his tongue from evil and his lips from speaking deceit; let him turn away from evil and do good; let him seek peace and pursue it."

Always converse with a level head, or you will make a bad situation worse.

Why is sarcasm harmful to successful communication?

Apply Bible principles from *Colossians 4:6 NCV*

When you talk, you should always be kind and pleasant so you will be able to answer everyone in the way you should.

Christians should avoid making sarcastic comments because it is rude and an example of bad manners.

Why should I taste my words before speaking them to my partner?

Apply Bible principles from *Ephesians 4:29 The Message*

Watch the way you talk. Let nothing foul or dirty come out of your mouth. Say only what helps, each word a gift.

Bitter words should leave an unpleasant taste in your mouth.

Why is it important to hear each other out in our conversations?

Apply Bible principles from *Proverbs 18:2 NCV*

Fools do not want to understand anything. They only want to tell others what they think.

It is not only important to hear our partner's point of view; it is also the respectful thing to do.

CHAPTER 5

Contentment

How can we be content no matter the circumstances? It is because we can rely on God's promises. *Matthew 6:30-32 (The Message) states, "If God gives such attention to the appearance of wildflowers—most of which are never even seen—don't you think he'll attend to you, take pride in you, do his best for you? What I'm trying to do here is to get you to relax, to not be so preoccupied with getting, so you can respond to God's giving. People who don't know God and the way he works fuss over these things, but you know both God and how he works. Steep your life in God-reality, God-initiative, God-provisions. Don't worry about missing out. You'll find all your everyday human concerns will be met."* This chapter focuses on being content knowing that if you seek first His kingdom and His righteousness, that all things will be given to you!

♥ ♥ ♥

What are the prime dating years of one's life?

Apply Bible principles from *Ecclesiastes 3:1–8 NIV*

For everything there is a season, and a time for every matter under heaven: a time to be born, and a time to die; a time to plant, and a time to pluck up what is planted; a time to kill, and a time to heal; a time to break down, and a time to build up; a time to weep, and a time to laugh; a time to mourn, and a time to dance; a time to cast away stones, and a time to gather stones together; a time to embrace, and a time to refrain from embracing; a time to search and a time to give up, a time to keep and a time to throw away, a time to tear and a time to mend, a time to be silent and a time to speak, a time to love and a time to hate, a time for war and a time for peace.

Scripture tells us there is a time for everything; even love. Keep praying and be patient. God will reveal everything he has for you in his own time. You only need to trust him.

Why are there both good and bad occurrences in relationships?

Apply Bible principles from *Ecclesiastes 7:14 The Message*

On a good day, enjoy yourself; on a bad day, examine your conscience. God arranges for both kinds of days so that we won't take anything for granted.

Enjoy the good times in your relationship and make a conscious effort to learn from the bad times. Continue to show gratitude to God for the many blessings bestowed upon you.

Why is a humble spirit a great asset in relationships?

Apply Bible principles from *Matthew 5:5 The Message*

You're blessed when you're content with just who you are—no more, no less. That's the moment you find yourselves proud owners of everything that can't be bought.

"True humility is not thinking less of yourself; it is thinking of yourself less." — C.S. Lewis

Is it possible for Christians to be content with what they have?

Apply Bible principles from *Philippians 4:11–13 the Message*

I am telling you this, but not because I need something. I have learned to be satisfied with what I have and with whatever happens. I know how to live when I am poor and when I have plenty. I have learned the secret of how to live through any kind of situation—when I have enough to eat or when I am hungry, when I have everything I need or when I have nothing. Christ is the one who gives me the strength I need to do whatever I must do.

As Christians, we should not focus on what we do not have. Instead, what we have to offer others should be our concern. Remember, possessions (material things) are not a guarantee for happiness or contentment.

Does it matter that my partner earns less than me?

Apply Bible principles from *Proverbs 28:6 ESV*

Better is a poor man who walks in his integrity than a rich man who is crooked in his ways.

Unfortunately, so much of the secular world focuses on money and material things. However, as a Christian, would you rather have a wealthy man who treats you poorly, or a man of modest means, who is God-fearing, treat you as a queen?

Is there such a thing as dating beneath me?

Apply Bible principles from *Romans 12:3 NLT*

Because of the privilege and authority God has given me, I give each of you this warning: Don't think you are better than you really are. Be honest in your evaluation of yourselves, measuring yourselves by the faith God has given us.

In the Bible, God instructs us to be humble and to think of others as better than ourselves. The dictionary defines humble as "having or showing a modest opinion or estimate of one's own importance." Bear this in mind when you experience those sinful feelings of superiority over others.

How can I keep my Christian relationship healthy?

Apply Bible principles from *Luke 6:37 ESV*

Judge not, and you will not be judged; condemn not, and you will not be condemned; forgive, and you will be forgiven.

The Bible tells us "all have sinned and fall short of the Glory of God." Therefore, we are not in any position to judge our partners. It is also wise to follow the golden rule and treat our partner as we would like to be treated.

CHAPTER 6

Discernment

As Christians, we should be very cautious of false teachings, non-biblical thinking and attitudes, and behavior that does not please God. Kenneth Copeland offers this unique quote on discernment, *"Sometimes you can tell what something is by what is isn't."* On your journey, stay committed to God's Word because it will always keep you on the righteous path that He has designed just for you.

♥   ♥   ♥

How can I tell if my partner is a committed Christian?

Apply Bible principles from *1 John 3:10 The Message*

People conceived and brought into life by God don't make a practice of sin. How could they? God's seed is deep within them, making them who they are. It's not in the nature of the God-begotten to practice and parade sin. Here's how you tell the difference between God's children and the Devil's children: The one who won't practice righteous ways isn't from God, nor is the one who won't love brother or sister. A simple test.

Being a Christian is established by how a person conducts his or her life. Christians should not walk in step with the wicked.

Why should I date someone who knows God's Word?

Apply Bible principles from *2 Timothy 3:16–17 NCV*

All Scripture is inspired by God and is useful for teaching, for showing people what is wrong in their lives, for correcting faults, and for teaching how to live right. Using the Scriptures, the person who serves God will be capable, having all that is needed to do every good work.

It helps when both people in the relationship speak the same spiritual language.

Why is The Book of Proverbs such a dynamic teaching tool for Christian relationships?

Apply Bible principles from *Proverbs 1:4 ERV*

They make the uneducated wise and give knowledge and sense to the young.

The Book of Proverbs is an excellent collection of moral instruction and spiritual wisdom. It presents a sensible, no-nonsense approach to conducting our daily lives as Christians. It also sheds light on social relationships, everyday etiquette, self-discipline, modesty, tolerance, and good manners.

How can we identify a true teacher of the Word?

Apply Bible principles from *Matthew 7:16–20 ERV*

You will know these people because of what they do. Good things don't come from people who are bad, just as grapes don't come from thorn bushes, and figs don't come from thorny weeds. In the same way, every good tree produces good fruit, and bad trees produce bad fruit. A good tree cannot produce bad fruit, and a bad tree cannot produce good fruit. Every tree that does not produce good fruit is cut down and thrown into the fire. You will know these false people by what they do.

"Preach the Gospel at all times, and when necessary, use words!"
— Francis of Assisi

Why should a Christian avoid a "smooth talker" as a mate?

Apply Bible principles from *Proverbs 26:23 The Message*

Smooth talk from an evil heart is like glaze on cracked pottery.

Remember, God knows our hearts, and will not only judge us by our acts, but by our thoughts and motivations as well. Make sure the intentions of your partner are authentic.

Are independent women problematic in Christian relationships?

Apply Bible principles from *1 Corinthians 11:11 NCV*

But in the Lord women are not independent of men, and men are not independent of women.

It is God's will that both men and women are equally dependent on each other. The Bible teaches that the woman originates from the rib of man, and the man is birthed through the womb of the women.

How can I best discern if my partner is a good person?

Apply Bible principles from *Luke 6:45 NLV*

Good comes from a good man because of the riches he has in his heart. Sin comes from a sinful man because of the sin he has in his heart. The mouth speaks of what the heart is full of.

A person's actions and behavior stem from what is inside his or her heart. It has nothing to do with what he or she professes to believe.

How can I determine if my partner is relationship worthy?

Apply Bible principles from *Proverbs 2:12–15 TNIV*

Wisdom will save you from the ways of wicked men, from men whose words are perverse, who have left the straight paths to walk in dark ways, who delight in doing wrong and rejoice in the perverseness of evil, whose paths are crooked and who are devious in their ways.

Your partner may not confess his or her feelings for you. So, pay closer attention to the actions than the spoken words.

CHAPTER 7

Emotional Concerns

An emotionally mature person is calm, considerate, focused, and decisive. This person is capable of managing stress, adept at controlling anger and proficient at reconciling disagreements with others. As Christians, we strive to keep a positive attitude even when faced with adverse circumstances. This chapter demonstrates how Christians should handle frustration and cope with anxiety within a relationship.

♥ ♥ ♥

Why is emotional maturity essential for a loving relationship?

Apply Bible principles from *Proverbs 29:11 ESV*

A fool gives full vent to his spirit, but a wise man quietly holds it back.

Inner peace happens when you do not allow people and circumstances to control your emotions.

Can jealousy ruin a Christian relationship?

Apply Bible principles from *Proverbs 14:30 NIV*

A heart at peace gives life to the body, but envy rots the bones.

Jealousy is a vicious poison and a threat to any healthy relationship.

What if my partner cannot control his or her emotions?

Apply Bible principles from *Proverbs 19:19 NIV*

A hot-tempered person must pay the penalty; rescue them, and you will have to do it again.

An adult with a bad temper is equivalent to a child having a tantrum. You may need to re-consider whether your mate is emotionally mature enough to sustain a healthy committed relationship.

Why should I feel empowered in a relationship?

Apply Bible principles from *2 Timothy 1:7 NCV*

God did not give us a spirit that makes us afraid but a spirit of power and love and self-control.

Our God will supply the strength needed to overcome all obstacles if we believe in him and keep his commandments.

How can feelings of envy affect a relationship?

Apply Bible principles from *Proverbs 27:4 ERV*

Anger is cruel and can destroy like a flood, but jealousy is much worse.

Remember, envy is a sin and bitterness usually follows close behind.

How can I conquer feelings of hopelessness in a relationship?

Apply Bible principles from *Psalms 34:17 NCV*

The Lord hears good people when they cry out to him, and he saves them from all their troubles.

When confronted with difficult situations, call on our Heavenly Father with expectation that your prayers are answered.

Will God help me handle my relationship frustrations?

Apply Bible principles from *Nahum 1:7 ERV*

The Lord is good. He is a safe place to go to in times of trouble. He takes care of those who trust him.

Quiet reflection and prayer are the best cures for controlling frustration in your life.

Why should we support each other in times of despair?

Apply Bible principles from *2 Corinthians 1:3–4 The Message*

All praise to the God and Father of our Master, Jesus the Messiah! Father of all mercy! God of all healing counsel! He comes alongside us when we go through hard times, and before you know it, he brings us alongside someone else who is going through hard times so that we can be there for that person just as God was there for us. We have plenty of hard times that come from following the Messiah, but no more so than the good times of his healing comfort—we get a full measure of that, too.

When we are compassionate toward each other, it helps us to overcome our own selfish needs.

How do I respond to an enraged partner?

Apply Bible principles from *Proverbs 15:1 NCV*

A gentle answer will calm a person's anger, but an unkind answer will cause more anger.

You are not accountable for the actions of others; however, you will have to give an account to God for your actions. Therefore, respond in kindness and compassion when confronted by an angry person. You can never know what an individual is experiencing in his or her life.

Why is losing control of my emotions destructive to a relationship?

Apply Bible principles from *Proverbs 14:17 The Message*

The hotheaded do things they'll later regret; the coldhearted get the cold shoulder.

When you lose control, you give up your power in the relationship!

Why is jealousy a deal-breaker in most relationships?

Apply Bible principles from *James 3:16 KJV*

For where envying and strife is, there is confusion and every evil work.

Jealousy can be a normal emotional response. However, how we react to jealousy can be problematic.

CHAPTER 8

Faith

The importance of sound faith is revealed in *Hebrews 11:6 (NIRV)* *"Without faith it isn't possible to please God. Those who come to God must believe that he exists. And they must believe that he rewards those who look to him."* Christians recognize that a compelling faith is essential in all aspects of our lives. This chapter highlights the significance of faith in our dating relationships.

Can my faith get me through the rough patches in a relationship?

Apply Bible principles from *Matthew 21:21 NCV*

Jesus answered, "I tell you the truth, if you have faith and do not doubt, you will be able to do what I did to this tree and even more. You will be able to say to this mountain, 'Go, fall into the sea.' And if you have faith, it will happen.

Strong faith is cultivated by obedience to God's word. Keep in mind, God sees, hears, and he will deliver.

Will the Lord send me a Christian mate?

Apply Bible principles from *Matthew 21:22 NLT*

You can pray for anything, and if you have faith, you will receive it.

The Lord will give you your heart's desire as long as you have faith and are obedient to His word. In the meantime, fall in love with God first, and he will give you the right person at just the right time.

Why should Christian men desire marriage?

Apply Bible principles from *Proverbs 18:22 ESV*

He who finds a wife finds a good thing and obtains favor from the Lord.

God created woman to be a companion to man. The Bible clearly advises "two people are better off than one, for they can help each other succeed."

Will I ever find a Christian mate to love me?

Apply Bible principles from *Psalms 31:24 NIV*

Be strong, all of you who put your hope in the Lord. Never give up.

God loves you! He will deliver whatever you need in his own time. You should never give up on God because he will never forsake you. Remember, worrying should end where your faith begins.

What should I do if I feel lost in a relationship?

Apply Bible principles from *Psalms 46:10 ESV*

Be still, and know that I am God....

Sometimes we just need to be still and listen for God's instructions!

Does it matter if my level of spiritual maturity exceeds my partner?

Apply Bible principles from *Romans 15:1 The Message*

Those of us who are strong and able in the faith need to step in and lend a hand to those who falter, and not just do what is most convenient for us. Strength is for service, not status. Each one of us needs to look after the good of the people around us, asking ourselves, "How can I help?"

Be patient! Everyone does not develop at the same pace spiritually.

How does the Lord know my needs in a Christian mate?

Apply Bible principles from *Matthew 6:8 The Message*

This is your Father you are dealing with, and he knows better than you what you need.

God sees and knows all things. Isn't it wonderful that our Heavenly Father knows more about our needs than we do and is, therefore, able to guide our steps?

Are the Bible's principles still relevant today?

Apply Bible principles from *Hebrews 4:12 ERV*

God's word is alive and working. It is sharper than the sharpest sword and cuts all the way into us. It cuts deep to the place where the soul and the spirit are joined. God's word cuts to the center of our joints and our bones. It judges the thoughts and feelings in our hearts.

The proof regarding the relevance of the Bible today lies in the blessings bestowed upon the people who follow its teachings.

How do I overcome my feelings of loneliness?

Apply Bible principles from *John 14:18 KJV*

I will not leave you comfortless: I will come to you.

Remember, dating is not a cure for loneliness – God is! It also helps to surround yourself with positive and supportive Christians who uplift you.

Why does the Lord correct our behavior?

Apply Bible principles from *Proverbs 3:12 ERV*

The Lord corrects the one he loves, just as a father corrects a child he cares about.

God corrects us because of his love for us. We should listen and heed His advice because blessings flow based on our obedience.

How do I move forward after heartbreak?

Apply Bible principles from *Proverbs 3:12 ERV*

But those who wait on the Lord shall renew their strength; they shall mount up with wings like eagles, they shall run and not be weary, they shall walk and not faint.

Daily devotionals enhance your faith and renew your strength.

How do I avoid rushing into love because I am lonely?

Apply Bible principles from *Song of Solomon 2:7 The Message*

Oh, let me warn you, sisters in Jerusalem, by the gazelles, yes, by all the wild deer: Don't excite love, don't stir it up, until the time is ripe—and you're ready.

It is very beneficial and rewarding to spend your leisure time carrying out the Lord's work, and not focusing solely on your love life. In the meantime, strengthen your relationship with God. Once you meet your Christian partner, you will realize that you enhance the relationship when you include God, and the relationship that excludes Him is worthless.

♥　♥　♥

CHAPTER 9

Fear

When trying to find love, oftentimes fear is the one obstacle holding us back from pursuing satisfying dating relationships. In fact, research shows that some of the major factors contributing and/or feeding relationship stumbling blocks are:

1. Fear of heartbreak
2. Afraid of losing his or her freedom
3. Terrified of trusting others
4. Fearful of rejection
5. Frightened of change

As Christians, we believe in the godly wisdom of *2 Timothy 1:7 (NIV) God did not give us a spirit that makes us afraid but a spirit of power and love and self-control.* This chapter explores how Christians should address common relationship fears.

♥   ♥   ♥

How can I overcome my fear of trusting others?

Apply Bible principles from *Psalms 56:3–4 ESV*

....

When I am afraid, I put my trust in you. In God, whose word I praise, in God I trust; I shall not be afraid. What can flesh do to me?

Placing your complete trust in God is life-changing. Allow him to direct your next steps in an effort to trust again.

How should I handle my fear of rejection in a relationship?

Apply Bible principles from *Psalms 27:10 NLT*

Even if my father and mother abandon me, the Lord will hold me close.

Just know that even though your fellow man may reject you, you are chosen and precious to God.

How should I cope with fear in a relationship?

Apply Bible principles from *Psalms 27:1–3 NLT*

The Lord is my light and my salvation—so why should I be afraid? The Lord is my fortress, protecting me from danger, so why should I tremble? When evil people come to devour me, when my enemies and foes attack me, they will stumble and fall. Though a mighty army surrounds me, my heart will not be afraid. Even if I am attacked, I will remain confident.

God is the only thing is this world worthy of fear.

As a victim of domestic violence, how do I move forward in a new relationship?

Apply Bible principles from *Psalms 9:9 The Message*

God's a safe-house for the battered, a sanctuary during bad times. The moment you arrive, you relax; you're never sorry you knocked.

Do not be defined by your wounds. Move on with your life and do not allow the past pain to restrict your future joy. Continue to make your relationship with God your highest priority, and he will provide the protection and strength you seek.

Why should I embrace change in a relationship?

Apply Bible principles from *Psalms 46:1–3 NCV*

God is our protection and our strength. He always helps in times of trouble. So we will not be afraid even if the earth shakes, or the mountains fall into the sea, even if the oceans roar and foam, or the mountains shake at the raging sea.

Change is an inevitable part of life. However, Scripture reminds us of God's unchanging presence in our lives.

How do I move beyond the bad relationships?

Apply Bible principles from *Philippians 3:13–14 NCV*

Brothers and sisters, I know that I have not yet reached that goal, but there is one thing I always do. Forgetting the past and straining toward what is ahead, I keep trying to reach the goal and get the prize for which God called me through Christ to the life above.

Look back and thank God – Look forward and trust God.

CHAPTER 10

Forgiveness

Forgiveness is essential in any successful relationship. Christians must forgive each other, although it is not always easy. Surprisingly, many Christians believe that forgiveness is something you do for the other person. But, the truth is, forgiveness is something we do for ourselves. It lightens our load and allows us to live less encumbered. Trust me, the more people you forgive, the better you will feel. Keep in mind, when you forgive, it does not change your past, but it will change your future! This chapter focuses on why we should forgive each other, how to avoid needless conflict, why forgiveness is vital to a relationship, and how to be more forgiving, and so forth

Should I avoid dating a Christian with a troubled past?

Apply Bible principles from *2 Corinthians 5:17 ESV*

Therefore, if anyone is in Christ, he is a new creation. The old has passed away; behold, the new has come.

Every Saint has a past just as every sinner has a future.

How can I forgive my partner after being verbally attacked?

Apply Bible principles from *Romans 12:17 NLT*

Never pay back evil for evil to anyone. Do things in such a way that everyone can see you are honorable.

Every time you overlook an offense and remain calm through calamity, you are proving to everyone that you serve a powerful God.

Why is forgiveness so vital in a Christian relationship?

Apply Bible principles from *Matthew 6:14 NLV*

For if you forgive other people when they sin against you, your Heavenly Father will also forgive you.

Forgive others so that God will forgive your transgressions.

How can I be more forgiving of my partner in a relationship?

Apply Bible principles from *Mark 11:25–26 ERV*

When you are praying and you remember that you are angry with another person about something, forgive that person. Forgive them so that your Father in heaven will also forgive your sins.

When you pray for someone who offends you, it helps you to understand why he or she behaves a certain way.

If I forgive my partner at least once, isn't that enough?

Apply Bible principles from *Matthew 18:21–22 The Message*

At that point Peter got up the nerve to ask, "Master, how many times I forgive a brother or sister who hurts me? Seven?" Jesus replied, "Seven! Hardly. Try seventy times seven."

It takes a strong Christian to apologize, and an even stronger Christian to forgive.

Isn't my partner off the hook if I keep forgiving him or her?

Apply Bible principles from *Matthew 6:14 ERV*

Don't be misled: No one makes a fool of God. What a person plants, he will harvest. The person who plants selfishness, ignoring the needs of others—ignoring God!—harvests a crop of weeds. All he'll have to show for his life is weeds! But the one who plants in response to God, letting God's Spirit do the growth work in him, harvests a crop of real life, eternal life.

God is in control, not you, so continue to be obedient to his word regardless of the circumstances.

How can I avoid needless conflict in a relationship?

Apply Bible principles from *Luke 6:3 NKJV*

Judge not, and you shall not be judged. Condemn not, and you shall not be condemned. Forgive, and you will be forgiven.

Learn to be selfless in your relationships. When you take the focus off of yourself, you will be amazed how quickly the conflicts dissolve.

How should I cope with guilt in a Christian relationship?

Apply Bible principles from *1 John 1:9 NCV*

But if we confess our sins, he will forgive our sins, because we can trust God to do what is right. He will cleanse us from all the wrongs we have done.

Always seek God's forgiveness, thereby eliminating the damaging guilt trips.

Should we admit our mistakes to each other in a relationship?

Apply Bible principles from *James 5:16 NCV*

Confess your sins to each other and pray for each other so God can heal you. When a believing person prays, great things happen.

When you make a mistake, admit the mistake, learn from it, and don't repeat the offense.

Have I really forgiven my partner if I cannot let the matter go?

Apply Bible principles from *Proverbs 17:9 ERV*

Forgive someone, and you will strengthen your friendship. Keep reminding them, and you will destroy it.

Remember, there is no love without forgiveness.

♥ ♥ ♥

CHAPTER 11

Guidance

Where would we be without the Holy Bible to guide our steps? So many times we struggle with matters in the world when all we have to do is turn to God's Word. Unfortunately, we sometimes think that we have a better answer. Christians must recognize that biblical Scripture will never lead us astray! Christian Evangelist Leonard Ravenhill quotes, "If you kneel before God you will stand before men!" This chapter highlights the need for spiritual guidance in our relationships.

♥ ♥ ♥

Should I seek godly counsel before making difficult decisions in a relationship?

Apply Bible principles from *Isaiah 42:16 KJV*

In all thy ways acknowledge him, and he shall direct thy paths.

Unfortunately, most of us will attempt our way of doing things, then after failing, we seek out God's counsel. The correct approach is to seek godly counsel first.

....

Why should I communicate daily with God about my concerns?

Apply Bible principles from *Psalms 55:17 ERV*

I speak to God morning, noon, and night. I tell him what upsets me, and he listens to me!

Regular communication with God strengthens your faith and keeps His word foremost in your thoughts.

In a Christian relationship, should we make time to pray together?

Apply Bible principles from *Matthew 18:20 ERV*

Yes, if two or three people are together believing in me, I am there with them.

Praying as a couple builds an exceptionally solid foundation.

Should we seek Christian counsel regarding our relationship?

Apply Bible principles from *Proverbs 12:15 The Message*

Fools are headstrong and do what they like; wise people take advice.

Christian advice is helpful in every aspect of our lives. However, it is essential to find a firm believer who knows God's Word, and will provide the necessary knowledge and direction.

Why is spiritual growth critical while in relationships?

Apply Bible principles from *1 Peter 2:2 (NIRV)*

Like babies that were just born, you should long for the pure milk of God's word. It will help you grow up as believers.

As an informed Christian, you are better equipped to handle life's problems with the knowledge of God's Word in you.

Why should we ask God to guide our relationships?

Apply Bible principles from *Proverbs 2:6–9 NLV*

For the Lord gives wisdom. Much learning and understanding come from His mouth. He stores up perfect wisdom for those who are right with Him. He is a safe-covering to those who are right in their walk. He watches over the right way, and He keeps safe the way of those who belong to Him. Then you will understand what is right and good, and right from wrong and you will know what you should do.

Know that God's Word will never steer you in the wrong direction.

Why should we stay connected to God's Word while dating?

Apply Bible principles from *Matthew 4:4 NIV*

Jesus answered, "It is written: 'Man shall not live on bread alone, but on every word that comes from the mouth of God.'"

Staying in God's Word keeps you equipped for any of life's unexpected misfortunes. Remember, if you stay ready, you do not have to get ready.

Should we seek godly counsel when a relationship is going well?

Apply Bible principles from *1 Chronicles 16:11 NIV*

Look to the Lord and his strength; seek his face always.

Maintaining a connection to God's Word will keep you linked to the spiritual vine. Seek His counsel when you encounter both good and bad times.

How can my partner and I become saved?

Apply Bible principles from *Romans 10:9–10 NIV*

If you confess with your mouth, 'Jesus is Lord,' and believe in your heart that God raised him from the dead, you will be saved. For it is with your heart that you believe and are justified, and it is with your mouth that you confess and are saved.

Being saved renews your mind so that you want to live in a way that honors God.

CHAPTER 12

Honesty

onesty and trust are the essentials of Christian dating relationships. However, many Christians struggle with honesty in their everyday lives. In *John 14:6 NIV* Jesus states, *"I am the way, and the truth, and the life."* Therefore, as followers of Christ, we must be truthful and honest in our interactions with our partner. Remember, honesty reflects our character, just as our conduct reflects our faith. This chapter focuses on the importance of honesty in a Christian relationship.

How will I know if my partner is an honest person?

Apply Bible principles from *Proverbs 13:5 NIV*

Those who do right hate what is false...

Observe how your partner conducts his or her life.

Why is dishonesty unhealthy in Christian relationships?

Apply Bible principles from *Proverbs 26:28 NIRV*

A tongue that tells lies hates the people it hurts. And words that seem to praise you destroy you.

Even a little white lie can destroy trust and cause irreparable damage to a relationship.

Should I reveal the truth about my past relationships?

Apply Bible principles from *Luke 6:31 ESV*

And as you wish that others would do to you, do so to them.

If you are truthful, it becomes part of your past; whereas, a lie becomes part of your future.

Can constructive criticism strengthen a relationship?

Apply Bible principles from *Proverbs 28:23 ERV*

Correct someone, and later they will thank you. That is much better than just saying something to be nice.

In relationships, constructive criticism can be a valuable tool for creating an even stronger bond between partners, as well as increasing the level of trust. Of course, both parties must have a firm grip on their egos.

Why should we fight fair in a Christian relationship?

Apply Bible principles from *Deuteronomy 16:20 ERV*

Goodness and Fairness! You must try very hard to be good and fair all the time...

Remember, no one wins if the relationship loses.

♥   ♥   ♥

CHAPTER 13

Inner Beauty

Isn't it strange that so much of the "secular" world focuses on the outer beauty of a person while the spiritual world highlights the inner beauty? As Christians, our attention is placed on the purity of our partner's heart. We all agree that a physical attraction does play a role when selecting a Christian mate. However, focusing on whether a person should drive a particular car, hold certain professional degrees, stand two inches taller or weigh ten pounds less, seems more world-focused than bible-based. Remember, when it comes to a mate, what exists externally is not nearly as important as what happens internally! This chapter focuses on the beauty that should be significant for Christians, from a biblical perspective

♥ ♥ ♥

What type of woman should a Christian man seek?

Apply Bible principles from *Proverbs 31:10 KJV*

Who can find a virtuous woman for her price is far above rubies.

Having an honorable Christian woman in your corner as you meander through life is truly a precious gift from God.

What type of woman should a Christian man avoid?

Apply Bible principles from *Proverbs 6:23–24 ERV*

Your parents give you commands and teachings that are like lights to show you the right way. This teaching corrects you and trains you to follow the path to life. It stops you from going to an evil woman, and it protects you from the smooth talk of another man's wife.

Listen to God for His guidance. It is very tempting to let our eyes select our mates. However, pray to God to send the right person into your life.

How should Christian women present themselves?

Apply Bible principles from *1 Peter 3:4 NIRV*

Instead, your beauty comes from inside you. It is the beauty of a gentle and quiet spirit. Beauty like that doesn't fade away. God places great value on it.

Beauty that radiates from within is the most inspiring kind.

How should a Christian woman dress?

Apply Bible principles from *1 Timothy 2 NIV*

I also want the women to dress modestly, with decency and propriety, adorning themselves, not with elaborate hairstyles or gold or pearls or expensive clothes, but with good deeds, appropriate for women who profess to worship God.

Modesty and decency speak to everyone about what lies on the inside of a woman.

What type of men should Christian women prefer?

Apply Bible principles from *Acts 13:22 NLT*

But God removed Saul and replaced him with David, a man about whom God said, 'I have found David, son of Jesse, a man after my own heart. He will do everything I want him to do.

You should focus on the Biblical definition of a "good" person, and not your own. After all, a man after God's own heart is a treasure to behold.

♥ ♥ ♥

CHAPTER 14

Joy

Count it all joy! Surprisingly, many Christians confuse happiness and joy. So, for the sake of clarification, happiness is influenced by external conditions and is temporary. It is unfortunate that most often happiness is dependent upon the behavior and actions of others. Whereas, on the other hand, joy is an internal condition and is unwavering. It represents our trust in God that he is controlling our situations. Therefore, we can release the reigns of worry, and continue to enjoy our lives. This chapter provides the clues to help you identify a healthy and cheerful connection.

♥ ♥ ♥

Are there ways to know if my partner is happy?

Apply Bible principles from *Proverbs 15:13 ESV*

A glad heart makes a cheerful face, but by sorrow of heart the spirit is crushed.

Always remember that the eyes are the window into the soul. It is also critical to observe body language, tone of voice, and facial expressions.

How should I embrace the positive moments in a relationship?

Apply Bible principles from *Ecclesiastes 9:7 The Message*

Seize life! Eat bread with gusto. Drink wine with a robust heart. Oh yes—God takes pleasure in your pleasure!

Appreciate and acknowledge the positive aspects of a relationship.

What are the advantages of a happy heart in a relationship?

Apply Bible principles from *Proverbs 17:22 NIRV*

A cheerful heart makes you healthy. But a broken spirit dries you up.

A happy heart is good medicine for the soul, and it creates a warm relationship environment.

Why should we motivate each other in a relationship?

Apply Bible principles from *Hebrews 10:24 NLT*

Let us think of ways to motivate one another to acts of love and good works.

Speaking to your partner in a manner that is kind and uplifting can be all the motivation he or she needs at that moment.

How can I maintain a joyous spirit while dating?

Apply Bible principles from *Psalm 1:1–3 NCV*

Happy are those who don't listen to the wicked, who don't go where sinners go, who don't do what evil people do. They love the Lord's teachings, and they think about those teachings day and night. They are strong, like a tree planted by a river. The tree produces fruit in season, and its leaves don't die. Everything they do will succeed.

Whenever your spirits are low seek out those who are in need of help. Serving others is a miracle drug that will never fail to uplift you.

♥   ♥   ♥

CHAPTER 15

Kindness

The basis of love is patience and kindness! As Christians, we should be kind to all, including our dating partners. Oftentimes it seems that we treat those closest to us the worst, even though the Bible explicitly instructs us otherwise. I think Mark Twain defines it best, *"Kindness is the language which the deaf can hear and the blind can see!"* This chapter emphasizes how an act of kindness can elevate your Christian relationships to the next level.

♥　♥　♥

Should we give generously to each other in a Christian relationship?

Apply Bible principles from *Matthew 10:8 KJV*

...Freely ye have received, freely give.

A selfless Christian does not have a problem sharing with others.

Why should my partner and I always respond with a positive attitude toward each other?

Apply Bible principles from *Timothy 2:24 ERV*

As a servant of the Lord, you must not argue. You must be kind to everyone. You must be a good teacher, and you must be patient.

A positive outlook will take us much further than a negative one.

Why is a kind heart an asset in a Christian relationship?

Apply Bible principles from *Proverbs 11:17 The Message*

When you're kind to others, you help yourself; when you're cruel to others, you hurt yourself.

A compassionate Christian expresses warmth, concern, consideration, and gentleness.

What is the most attractive trait in a Christian man?

Apply Bible principles from *Proverbs 19:22 NASB*

What is desirable in a man is his kindness...

Kindness goes a long way in a relationship. Do not underestimate the power of a caring heart.

How beneficial is a tender greeting extended to my partner?

Apply Bible principles from *2 Samuel 15:5–6 The Message*

Whenever someone would treat him with special honor, he'd shrug it off and treat him like an equal, making him feel important. Absalom did this to everyone who came to do business with the king and stole the hearts of everyone in Israel.

Treat your loved ones as you would treat a fragile package; handle with care.

Why is expressing compassion towards others essential?

Apply Bible principles from *Hebrews 13:1–3 NCV*

Keep on loving each other as brothers and sisters. Remember to welcome strangers, because some who have done this have welcomed angels without knowing it. Remember those who are in prison as if you were in prison with them. Remember those who are suffering as if you were suffering with them

Christians must show compassion to all because we never know how heavy a burden someone may be carrying.

How should Christians treat an ungrateful partner?

Apply Bible principles from *Luke 6:27–36 The Message*

But I say to you who are listening, love your enemies. Do good to those who hate you, bless those who curse you, pray for those who are cruel to you. If anyone slaps you on one cheek, offer him the other cheek, too. If someone takes your coat, do not stop him from taking your shirt. Give to everyone who asks you, and when someone takes something that is yours, don't ask for it back. Do to others what you would want them to do to you. If you love only the people who love you, what praise should you get? Even sinners love the people who love them. If you do good only to those who do good to you, what praise should you get? Even sinners do that! If you lend things to people, always hoping to get something back, what praise should you get? Even sinners lend to other sinners so that they can get back the same amount. But love your enemies, do good to them, and lend to them without hoping to get anything back. Then you will have a great reward, and you will be children of the Most High God, because he is kind even to people who are ungrateful and full of sin. Show mercy, just as your Father shows mercy.

Be kind to all. Remember, hurting people tend to hurt other people.

How does God want us to behave toward each other?

Apply Bible principles from *Colossians 3:12 NASB*

So, as those who have been chosen of God, holy and beloved, put on a heart of compassion, kindness, humility, gentleness and patience.

Let you partner know that he or she is a special person in your life.

Why should we give to each other freely and cheerfully?

Apply Bible principles from *2 Corinthians 9:7 ERV*

Each one of you should give what you have decided in your heart to give. You should not give if it makes you unhappy or if you feel forced to give. God loves those who are happy to give.

Giving from the heart is very rewarding.

How should a Christian woman communicate?

Apply Bible principles from *Proverbs 31:26 The Message*

When she speaks she has something worthwhile to say, and she always says it kindly.

A kind and gentle woman is a treasure to behold.

Why is timing so significant when communicating?

Apply Bible principles from *Proverbs 25:11 ERV*

Saying the right thing at the right time is like a golden apple in a silver setting.

The mood of the listener can also affect the outcome of the communication. Therefore, watch your tone, as well as your words, avoid interruptions, and stick to current matters without bringing up the past. Avoid aggressive behavior.

What are the benefits of always doing right towards one another?

Apply Bible principles from *Galatians 6:9 NIV*

Let us not become weary in doing good, for at the proper time we will reap a harvest if we do not give up.

As a Christian, doing good should make you feel good.

CHAPTER 16

Love

L ove is the single most powerful emotion! The biblical definition of love is provided in *1 Corinthians 13:4-7 (ERV)*, "*Love is patient and kind. Love is not jealous, it does not brag, and it is not proud. Love is not rude, it is not selfish, and it cannot be made angry easily. Love does not remember wrongs done against it. Love is never happy when others do wrong, but it is always happy with the truth. Love never gives up on people. It never stops trusting, never loses hope, and never quits.*" This chapter focuses on the importance of a loving Christian relationship and how it affects every area of our lives. Some of the relevant questions include, are there ways to know if my partner loves me? How do I recover from heartbreak? What if my partner does not believe in love? Do Christian men love as deeply as Christian women?

♥　♥　♥

How should I express my feelings to my partner?

Apply Bible principles from *Romans 12:9 The Message MSG*

Love from the center of who you are; don't fake it. Run for dear life from evil; hold on for dear life to good. Be good friends who love deeply; practice playing second fiddle.

If you always have a motive of love, expressing love will come naturally.

How can I tell if my partner truly loves the Lord?

Apply Bible principles from *John 14:15 ESV*

If you love me, you will keep my commandments.

A person's behavior, or obedience to God's word, will always tell you if he or she loves the Lord.

Are there ways to know if my partner loves me?

Apply Bible principles from *1 Corinthians 13:4–7 NIV*

Love is patient, love is kind. It does not envy, it does not boast, it is not proud. It does not dishonor others, it is not self-seeking, it is not easily angered, it keeps no record of wrongs. Love does not delight in evil but rejoices with the truth. It always protects, always trusts, always hopes, always perseveres.

Listen to what your partner says, and most important, how he or she treats you.

How can we keep a Christian relationship fresh and invigorating?

Apply Bible principles from *1 Peter 4:8 NLT*

Most important of all, continue to show deep love for each other, for love covers a multitude of sins.

We should explore new ways to express love and kindness to each other.

Do Christian men love as deeply as Christian women?

Apply Bible principles from *Genesis 29:20 NLT*

So Jacob served seven years for Rachel, and they seemed to him but a few days because of the love he had for her.

In relationship communications, women need to hear the love; men need to hear the respect.

Is it naïve to believe love still exists in relationships?

Apply Bible principles from *1 Corinthians 13:13 NCV*

So these three things continue forever: faith, hope, and love. And the greatest of these is love.

The Bible clearly states, "Without love, you have nothing."

What if my partner does not believe in love?

Apply Bible principles from *1 John 4:8 NKJV*

He who does not love does not know God, for God is love.

It is wise to date someone who shares the same faith and beliefs.

How do I keep a Christian relationship energized?

Apply Bible principles from *1 Corinthians 16:14 NCV*

Do everything in love.

Always keep your partner's best interests at heart.

Why should we support each other spiritually?

Apply Bible principles from *Hebrews 10:24 ESV*

And let us consider how to stir up one another to love and good works.

Spiritual support will strengthen the bond you share.

What is the golden rule for a great relationship?

Apply Bible principles from *Luke 6:31 NIRV*

Do to others as you want them to do to you.

It is simple, treat your partner the way you would like to be treated!

How important is love in my life?

Apply Bible principles from *1 Corinthians 13:1–3 ESV*

If I speak in the tongues of men and of angels, but have not love, I am a noisy gong or a clanging cymbal. And if I have prophetic powers, and understand all mysteries and all knowledge, and if I have all faith, so as to remove mountains, but have not love, I am nothing. If I give away all I have, and if I deliver up my body to be burned, but have not love, I gain nothing.

Always remember that God's love is the ultimate love.

Is there a right time for love in a Christian's life?

Apply Bible principles from *Song of Songs 3:5 NIV*

Daughters of Jerusalem, I charge you by the gazelles and by the does of the field: Do not arouse or awaken love until it so desires.

We should always trust God's timing.

How do I recover from heartbreak?

Apply Bible principles from *Psalms 147:3 NIV*

He heals the broken-hearted and binds up their wounds.

If you want to mend a broken heart, you must give God all the pieces.

How important is hospitality among partners in a Christian relationship?

Apply Bible principles from *Romans 12:13 NLT*

When God's people are in need, be ready to help them. Always be eager to practice hospitality.

We should treat our partner as an honored guest.

How do we demonstrate our Christian support for each other?

Apply Bible principles from *Romans 12:15 NCV*

Be happy with those who are happy, and be sad with those who are sad.

We should sympathize and empathize with our partner when appropriate.

What is the basis of Christian love?

Apply Bible principles from *1 Corinthians 13:4 ESV*

Love is patient and kind.

Keep this verse in the forefront of your mind when interacting with your partner.

Why is self-centeredness unacceptable Christian relationship behavior?

Apply Bible principles from *Philippians 2:3 ERV*

In whatever you do, don't let selfishness or pride be your guide. Be humble, and honor others more than yourselves.

Selfishness is not an attractive trait in a Christian man or a woman.

How should Christians greet each other in a relationship?

Apply Bible principles from *1 Peter 5:14 NLT*

Greet each other with Christian Love.

When you greet your partner, pretend he or she is wearing a sign that says, "I want to feel special."

How can we keep the warmth in a Christian relationship?

Apply Bible principles from *1 Peter 3:8 The Message*

Be agreeable, be sympathetic, be loving, be compassionate, be humble.

We should always operate from a motive of love.

Why is competition discouraged amongst partners in a Christian relationship?

Apply Bible principles from *Galatians 6:4–5 ERV*

Don't compare yourself with others. Just look at your own work to see if you have done anything to be proud of. You must each accept the responsibilities that are yours.

When we compete against our mate, we build walls instead of bridges.

♥　♥　♥

CHAPTER 17

Obedience

Christians understand that our submission to God's Word brings forth blessings. We can confirm this in Romans 2:6-8 (ERV) *He will reward or punish everyone for what they have done. Some people live for God's glory, for honor, and for life that cannot be destroyed. They live for those things by always continuing to do good. God will give eternal life to them. But others are selfish and refuse to follow truth. They follow evil. God will show his anger and punish them.* This chapter poses pertinent relationship questions, such as, prior to marriage, how should I spend my single years? I am a faithful Christian, so why am I still single? How will I know if my partner is disobedient to God?

♥ ♥ ♥

Is it wrong for a Christian to date a legally separated person?

Apply Bible principles from *1 Corinthians 7:2 ESV*

But because of the temptation to sexual immorality, each man should have his own wife and each woman her own husband.

A legally separated person is married! Christians should not entertain the idea of dating the husband or wife of another person.

How will I know if my partner is disobedient to God?

Apply Bible principles from *2 Timothy 3:5 ERV*

They will go on pretending to be devoted to God, but they will refuse to let that "devotion" change the way they live. Stay away from these people!

Regardless of what you are being told, be mindful of how your potential partner conducts his or her life. It is not enough to be a Christian in name only; one must also submit to the lifestyle.

What if my partner does not obey all of God's rules?

Apply Bible principles from *James 2:10 NLT*

For the person who keeps all of the laws except one is as guilty as a person who has broken all of God's laws.

No one can claim to be a true Christian while selecting the laws of God he or she chooses to follow.

What is sound advice for Christian relationships?

Apply Bible principles from *Proverbs 2:11 NCV*

Good sense will protect you; understanding will guard you.

We should seek, as well as speak the truth when communicating with our partners.

Why should I watch my words when communicating with my partner?

Apply Bible principles from *1 Peter 3:10 NLT*

If you want to enjoy life and see many happy days, keep your tongue from speaking evil and your lips from telling lies.

Keep in mind, men prefer to use non-verbal cues when communicating; women prefer verbal methods to express thoughts and feelings.

Prior to marriage, how should I spend my single years?

Apply Bible principles from *1 Corinthians 7:34 NCV*

A woman who is not married or a girl who has never married is busy with the Lord's work. She wants to be holy in body and spirit.

Use your time as a single person to imitate the behavior of Christ by serving others. After all, this is one of the finest ways to honor God.

How can I enhance my spiritual growth?

Apply Bible principles from *Psalms 119:11 The Message*

How can a young person live a clean life? By carefully reading the map of your Word. I'm single-minded in pursuit of you; don't let me miss the road signs you've posted. I've banked your promises in the vault of my heart so I won't sin myself bankrupt. Be blessed, GOD; train me in your ways of wise living. I'll transfer to my lips all the counsel that comes from your mouth; I delight far more in what you tell me about living than in gathering a pile of riches. I ponder every morsel of wisdom from you, I attentively watch how you've done it. I relish everything you've told me of life, I won't forget a word of it.

A wise Christian should develop a daily prayer routine.

I am a faithful Christian, so why am I still single?

Apply Bible principles from *1 Corinthians 7:32 The Message*

I want you to live as free of complications as possible. When you're unmarried, you're free to concentrate on simply pleasing the Master. Marriage involves you in all the nuts and bolts of domestic life and in wanting to please your spouse, leading to so many more demands on your attention. The time and energy that married people spend on caring for and nurturing each other, the unmarried can spend in becoming whole and holy instruments of God. I'm trying to be helpful and make it as easy as possible for you, not make things harder. All I want is for you to be able to develop a way of life in which you can spend plenty of time together with the Master without a lot of distractions.

God has a purpose and a plan that will be revealed to you at the appropriate time. Be still and wait on the Lord.

How do I respond to those opposing my obedience to God's word?

Apply Bible principles from *1 Peter 3:13–16 The Message*

If with heart and soul you're doing good, do you think you can be stopped? Even if you suffer for it, you're still better off. Don't give the opposition a second thought. Through thick and thin, keep your hearts at attention, in adoration before Christ, your Master. Be ready to speak up and tell anyone who asks why you're living the way you are, and always with the utmost courtesy. Keep a clear conscience before God so that when people throw mud at you, none of it will stick. They'll end up realizing that they're the ones who need a bath. It's better to suffer for doing good, if that's what God wants, than to be punished for doing bad.

When the enemy knocks, let Jesus answer! Love and obey God without reservation or explanations.

♥ ♥ ♥

CHAPTER 18

Pain

Although unfortunate, most people involved in dating relationships will eventually encounter an emotionally painful experience. However, we should always keep the faith knowing that God will provide comfort for our heartbreaks. This chapter focuses on how we, as Christians, should manage these difficult circumstances. A few of the questions presented are, will God help the brokenhearted heal? Why is there sadness in relationships? How do I handle rejection in relationships?

Will God help the brokenhearted heal?

Apply Bible principles from *Psalms 34:18 NIRV*

The Lord is close to those whose hearts have been broken. He saves those whose spirits have been crushed.

You will need to open yourself up to God so that he can heal the pain you feel within. Trust in the Lord with all your heart.

Why is there sadness in relationships?

Apply Bible principles from *James 1:2–4 ERV*

My brothers and sisters, you will have many kinds of trouble. But this gives you a reason to be very happy. You know that when your faith is tested, you learn to be patient in suffering. If you let that patience work in you, the end result will be good. You will be mature and complete. You will be all that God wants you to be.

Use your pain to strengthen your faith! The pain you feel today will strengthen you for tomorrow's challenges.

How do I handle rejection in a relationship?

Apply Bible principles from *Psalms 27:10 NLT*

Even if my father and mother abandon me, the LORD will hold me close.

Rejection is God's way of re-directing you to something better.

Is a bitter heart capable of loving others?

Apply Bible principles from *Proverbs 14:10 NIV*

Each heart knows its own bitterness, and no one else can share its joy.

The only cure for a bitter heart is forgiveness of the person that brought on the pain. We must remain prayerful and allow God to soften our hearts.

Why should Christians not seek revenge in a relationship?

Apply Bible principles from *Proverbs 20:22 ESV*

Do not say, "I will repay evil"; wait for the Lord, and he will deliver you.

As Christians, we should seek God not revenge. We should not hide vengeful anger in our hearts.

How do I overcome my hurt feelings in a relationship?

Apply Bible principles from *Romans 5:3–5 NIV*

More than that, we rejoice in our sufferings, knowing that suffering produces endurance, and endurance produces character, and character produces hope, and hope does not put us to shame, because God's love has been poured into our hearts through the Holy Spirit who has been given to us.

Be prayerful that you are able to learn from the pain and move on with your life. As a Christian, you must remember that your strength lies in your relationship with your God.

♥ ♥ ♥

CHAPTER 19

Patience

When problems arise in the relationship, we should take the predicament to God first. If we follow this path, we do not direct our anger toward our family, friends or our partners. In addition, when we are impatient with our mate, we should stop and consider how patient God has been with each of us. This chapter emphasizes the power of tolerance in a Christian dating relationship. Some of the questions are, how critical is patience in a Christian relationship? Will patience help eliminate some of the problems in a relationship? Why is tolerance for each other beneficial in a relationship?

♥ ♥ ♥

How can I avoid becoming too anxious for a relationship?

Apply Bible principles from *Romans 8:25 NLT*

But if we look forward to something we don't yet have, we must wait patiently and confidently.

Demonstrate your faith by allowing yourself to wait on God's timing; not your own! Remember, a Christian woman who walks in purpose will never have to pursue a relationship.

How can I avoid becoming frustrated waiting for the right mate?

Apply Bible principles from *Isaiah 40:29 NIRV*

He gives strength to those who are tired. He gives power to those who are weak.

Never consider that your situation is hopeless because this indicates a lack of faith in God.

Has God forgotten about my desire to marry?

Apply Bible principles from *Psalms 27:14 KJV*

Wait on the LORD: be of good courage, and he shall strengthen thine heart: wait, I say, on the Lord.

When you are feeling doubtful, call on your faith to restore your confidence. God is always with you and will never forsake you.

How critical is patience in a Christian relationship?

Apply Bible principles from *Proverbs 25:15 The Message*

Patient persistence pierces through indifference; gentle speech breaks down rigid defenses.

When you are feeling impatient with your mate, take it to the Lord in prayer. The message in Scripture will always help you to overcome the obstacles you may face.

Why should I continue to wait for love?

Apply Bible principles from *Proverbs 19:2 ERV*

Being excited about something is not enough. You must also know what you are doing. Don't rush into something, or you might do it wrong.

You cannot manipulate the timing of God's master plan.

Will patience help to eliminate some of the problems in a relationship?

Apply Bible principles from Ecclesiastes 7:8 ESV

Better is the end of a thing than its beginning, and the patient in spirit is better than the proud in spirit.

Patience is about awaiting God's timing as well as trusting God's love.

Why is tolerance for each other helpful in a relationship?

Apply Bible principles from *Ephesians 4:2 NLT*

Always be humble and gentle. Be patient with each other, making allowances for each other's faults because of your love.

Tolerance expresses a need to understand the other person's point of view.

How should I nurture a healthy relationship?

Apply Bible principles from *Colossians 3:12–14 NASB*

So, as those who have been chosen of God, holy and beloved, put on a heart of compassion, kindness, humility, gentleness and patience; bearing with one another, and forgiving each other, whoever has a complaint against anyone; just as the Lord forgave you, so also should you. Beyond all these things put on love, which is the perfect bond of unity.

A caring and nurturing relationship needs the commitment and attention of both parties involved. No relationship can survive from the efforts of only one person.

How can I avoid being overly sensitive while communicating?

Apply Bible principles from *Proverbs 19:11 NCV*

Those who love your teachings will find true peace, and nothing will defeat them.

Be careful that you do not let negative emotions cloud your judgment when communicating. In other words, do not allow others to pull you into their storm; instead, you draw them into your calm.

♥ ♥ ♥

CHAPTER 20

Peace

Always strive for peace and tranquility in your dating relationships. Despite the popular belief, this sense of serenity is attainable even though it seems hopeless at times. A surefire way to achieve a peaceful relationship is by first securing an inner peace. However, this inner harmony emerges only after you build a meaningful relationship with Christ. This chapter emphasizes the value of peace in your relationships and asks questions, such as, is keeping the peace critical in a relationship? Why should I remain positive when feeling negative? How can I experience a harmonious relationship?

♥ ♥ ♥

How can I experience a harmonious relationship?

Apply Bible principles from *James 3:18 ERV*

People who work for peace in a peaceful way get the blessings that come from right living.

Harmony begins with you.

How can I avoid being anxious about falling in love?

Apply Bible principles from *Philippians 4:6–7 NLT*

Don't worry about anything; instead, pray about everything. Tell God what you need, and thank him for all he has done. Then you will experience God's peace, which exceeds anything we can understand. His peace will guard your hearts and minds as you live in Christ Jesus.

Worrying does not take away your troubles; it takes away your inner peace.

Is keeping the peace critical in a Christian relationship?

Apply Bible principles from *Ephesians 4:3 NLT*

Make every effort to keep yourselves united in the Spirit, binding yourselves together with peace.

Inner peace begets outer peace.

Why should I remain positive when I am feeling negative in a relationship?

Apply Bible principles from *Proverbs 15:15 The Message*

A miserable heart means a miserable life; a cheerful heart fills the day with song.

You cannot create a positive life with a negative mindset.

What are the benefits of being a peacemaker in a relationship?

Apply Bible principles from *James 3:18 NLT*

And those who are peacemakers will plant seeds of peace and reap a harvest of righteousness.

Those who are able to negotiate peace possess a sense of serenity envied by all.

How important is happiness in a relationship?

Apply Bible principles from *Ecclesiastes 3:12 NCV*

So I realize that the best thing for them is to be happy and enjoy themselves as long as they live.

A blissful atmosphere combats the stress and tension in your life. Every time you find delight in a challenging situation you are victorious.

How can we empower each other in a Christian relationship?

Apply Bible principles from *Ephesians 4:29 NCV*

When you talk, do not say harmful things, but say what people need— words that will help others become stronger. Then what you say will do good to those who listen to you.

There is no better exercise than lifting each other up with words, affirmations, and prayer.

What is the function of a peacemaker in a relationship?

Apply Bible principles from *Matthew 5:9 The Message*

You're blessed when you can show people how to cooperate instead of compete or fight. That's when you discover who you really are, and your place in God's family.

As Christians, we should do everything we can to be at peace or make peace with one another.

♥ ♥ ♥

CHAPTER 21

Prayer

Never underestimate the power of prayer! In any relationship, especially a Christian dating relationship, we should never stop praying. Another positive is that the two of you can pray together. The benefit of a praying partner is demonstrated in Matthew 18:20 (NIV) *For where two or three gather in my name, there am I with them.* This chapter focuses on prayer in relationships. The questions presented include, should I pray for a Christian husband? Should we pray together for a blessed relationship? Will God answer my prayers for a godly husband?

♥ ♥ ♥

Should I pray for a Christian husband?

Apply Bible principles from *John 15:7 NLV*

But if you remain in me and my words remain in you, you may ask for anything you want, and it will be granted!

After praying, remember to listen for an answer from God.

....

Should we pray together for a blessed relationship?

Apply Bible principles from *Matthew 18:19 ESV*

Again I say to you, if two of you agree on earth about anything they ask, it will be done for them by my Father in heaven.

It is quite moving to hear your partner praying for you and the success of the relationship.

Why is daily prayer significant in Christian relationships?

Apply Bible principles from *Colossians 4:2 ERV*

Never stop praying. Be ready for anything by praying and being thankful.

When you make a commitment to a daily prayer ritual, you are demonstrating your dedication to our heavenly father.

Will God answer my prayers for a godly husband?

Apply Bible principles from *Psalms 84:11 ESV*

For the Lord God is a sun and shield; the Lord bestows favor and honor. No good thing does he withhold from those who walk uprightly.

Obedience to God brings forth blessings from Him.

Is it important to give thanks during the difficult times in a relationship?

Apply Bible principles from *1 Thessalonians 5:18 The Message*

Be cheerful no matter what; pray all the time; thank God no matter what happens. This is the way God wants you who belong to Christ Jesus to live.

When times are difficult, it takes great faith to give thanks for our situation. However, we should remember that we walk by faith—not by sight.

♥   ♥   ♥

CHAPTER 22

Respect

I t is rare that a dating relationship will survive without mutual respect for one another. You must respect yourself, your partner, and the relationship—and your partner must do the same! This chapter asks pertinent questions, such as, how does a Christian woman earn a Christian man's respect? How can I communicate respectfully a Christian relationship?

♥　♥　♥

How does a Christian woman earn a Christian man's respect?

Apply Bible principles from *Proverbs 11:16 NIRV*

A woman who has a kind heart gains respect…

Remember, respecting yourself encourages others to respect you.

What does the Bible say about respecting each other?

Apply Bible principles from *James 2:9 NLV*

But if you look on one man as more important than another, you are sinning. And the Law says you are sinning.

Christians should respect others because God has instructed us to through Scripture.

What if my partner has not earned my respect in a relationship?

Apply Bible principles from *1 Peter 2:17 NLT*

Respect everyone, and love your Christian brothers and sisters.

The bible instructs us to maintain an attitude of respect for everyone whether justified or not.

How can I communicate respectfully in a Christian relationship?

Apply Bible principles from *Proverbs 15:28 NLT*

The heart of the godly thinks carefully before speaking.

Always speak in a kind and gentle way.

CHAPTER 23

Sexual Purity

Sexual purity is about more than abstaining from sex. In fact, according to the Bible, purity involves keeping our hearts, minds (thoughts) and bodies holy and without moral blemish for the purposes of being obedient to God's word. Unfortunately, research has shown that keeping ourselves sexually pure is a major obstacle in many Christian relationships. This chapter highlights the principles in scripture related to sexual purity and asks questions, such as, where does sexual temptation come from? Can sinful thoughts damage a Christian relationship? How do I handle sexual temptation in a Christian relationship? Is it possible to stop having sex in a relationship? What if my partner insists on having sex with me?

♥　♥　♥

How can I remain sexually pure in a Christian relationship?

Apply Bible principles from *Matthew 26:41 ESV*

Watch and pray that you may not enter into temptation. The spirit indeed is willing, but the flesh is weak.

....

There are many worldly temptations to draw our attention away from God's Word. As Christians, the goal is to stay focused and prayerful so that we remain obedient.

How do I handle sexual temptation in a Christian relationship?

Apply Bible principles from *James 1:12 ESV*

So I tell you, live the way the Spirit leads you. Then you will not do the evil things your sinful self wants.

Stay away from the people, places, and activities that may make you vulnerable.

What is the difference between love and sex?

Apply Bible principles from *1 Corinthians 13:4–8 The Message*

Love never gives up. Love cares more for others than for self. Love doesn't want what it doesn't have. Love doesn't strut, Doesn't have a swelled head, Doesn't force itself on others, Isn't always "me first," Doesn't fly off the handle, Doesn't keep score of the sins of others, Doesn't revel when others grovel, Takes pleasure in the flowering of truth, Puts up with anything, Trusts God always, Always looks for the best, Never looks back, But keeps going to the end. Love never dies.

Love is an emotional feeling — sex is a physical act.

Where does sexual temptation come from?

Apply Bible principles from *James 1:14–15 The Message*

Don't let anyone under pressure to give in to evil say, "God is trying to trip me up." God is impervious to evil, and puts evil in no one's way. The temptation to give in to evil comes from us and only us. We have no one to blame but the leering, seducing flare-up of our own lust. Lust gets pregnant, and has a baby: sin! Sin grows up to adulthood, and becomes a real killer.

Your strong desires have become toxic when they interfere with your ability to serve God.

What are the benefits of practicing abstinence in a Christian relationship?

Apply Bible principles from *James 1:12 NLT*

God blesses those who patiently endure testing and temptation. Afterward they will receive the crown of life that God has promised to those who love him.

Those who are tempted and remain obedient will receive many blessings from God.

Can sinful thoughts damage a Christian relationship?

Apply Bible principles from *Romans 8:5 NIRV*

Don't live under the control of your sinful nature. If you do, you will think about what your sinful nature wants. Live under the control of the Holy Spirit. If you do, you will think about what the Spirit wants.

Sinful thoughts lead to sinful actions. Remember, your heart, mind (thoughts), and bodies should remain untarnished.

Is it ever too late to start practicing abstinence?

Apply Bible principles from *1 Peter 4:3 CEB*

You have wasted enough time doing what unbelievers desire—living in their unrestrained immorality and lust, their drunkenness and excessive feasting and wild parties, and their forbidden worship of idols.

It is never too late to commit to the life God wants you to live.

How do I respond to my friends who disapprove of my sexual purity pledge?

Apply Bible principles from *1 Peter 4:4–5 The Message Of course, your old friends don't understand why you don't join in with the old gang anymore. But you don't have to give an account to them. They're the ones who will be called on the carpet—and before God himself.*

Your real friends will always want the absolute best for you.

Why should I make a commitment to sexual purity?

Apply Bible principles from *1 Thessalonians 4:1–5 The Message*

One final word, friends. We ask you—urge is more like it—that you keep on doing what we told you to do to please God, not in a dogged religious plod, but in a living, spirited dance. You know the guidelines we laid out for you from the Master Jesus. God wants you to live a pure life. Keep yourselves from sexual promiscuity. Learn to appreciate and give dignity to your body, not abusing it, as is so common among those who know nothing of God.

It is God's will for you to live a wholesome life.

Why should I ignore peer pressure regarding my abstinence pledge?

Apply Bible principles from *Exodus 23:2 NCV*

You must not do wrong just because everyone else is doing it.

Your commitment is between you and God; not between you and your friends.

What if my partner insists on having sex with me?

Apply Bible principles from *1 Corinthians 5:11 NLV*

What I wrote was that you should not keep on being with a person who calls himself a Christian if he does any kind of sexual sins.

Your partner's actions need to be consistent with his or her beliefs. Someone who claims to be a Christian and yet behaving in a manner contrary to moral, biblical teachings is a fraud.

Is it possible to stop having sex in a relationship?

Apply Bible principles from *1 Corinthians 10:13 The Message*

No test or temptation that comes your way is beyond the course of what others have had to face. All you need to remember is that God will never let you down; he'll never let you be pushed past your limit; he'll always be there to help you come through it.

God will never put more on you than you can handle. Stay prayerful.

Why are sexual sins different from other sins?

Apply Bible principles from *1 Corinthians 6:18–20 The Message*

There's more to sex than mere skin on skin. Sex is as much spiritual mystery as physical fact. As written in Scripture, "The two become one." Since we want to become spiritually one with the Master, we must not pursue the kind of sex that avoids commitment and intimacy, leaving us more lonely than ever—the kind of sex that can never "become one." There is a sense in which sexual sins are different from all others. In sexual sin, we violate the sacredness of our own bodies, these bodies that were made for God-given and God-modeled love, for "becoming one" with another. Or didn't you realize that your body is a sacred place, the place of the Holy Spirit? Don't you see that you can't live however you please, squandering what God paid such a high price for? The physical part of you is not some piece of property belonging to the spiritual part of you. God owns the whole works. So let people see God in and through your body.

Remember, your body is your temple and deserves much respect.

What should I do if I have already sinned sexually in the relationship?

Apply Bible principles from *1 John 1:9 ERV*

But if we confess our sins, God will forgive us. We can trust God to do this. He always does what is right. He will make us clean from all the wrong things we have done.

When you call on the mighty name of Jesus, all things are possible! You can always pray and seek God's forgiveness for any offenses.

Will my partner wait until marriage to have sex?

Apply Bible principles from *1 Corinthians 13:4 NASB*

Love is patient!

If your partner is similarly committed to God's Word as you are, then your request to wait will be honored.

CHAPTER 24

Trust

Trust is one of the components of a meaningful relationship. However, most people, including Christians, have issues with trusting others. So as you meet potential partners, you should allow yourself ample time to establish the trustworthiness of your prospective mate. Once you are able to confirm that your partner is an honest person, then you can begin to open your heart to release love, as well as receive love from your partner. Again, always believe in God and follow his Word for support. This chapter addresses the issue of trust in Christian dating relationships.

♥ ♥ ♥

How will I know if my partner can be trusted with my heart?

Apply Bible principles from *Luke 16:10 ERV*

Whoever can be trusted with small things can also be trusted with big things. Whoever is dishonest in little things will be dishonest in big things, too. If you cannot be trusted with worldly riches, you will not be trusted with the true riches. And if you cannot be trusted with the things that belong to someone else, you will not be given anything of your own.

Always spend an adequate amount of time getting to know the person in the early stages of a relationship. This will increase your chances of determining his or her trustworthiness.

How do I remain strong when faced with adversity in a relationship?

Apply Bible principles from *Isaiah 12:2 The Message*

Yes, indeed—God is my salvation I trust, I won't be afraid. God—yes God!—is my strength and song, best of all, my salvation!

God is your strength, and your fortress. Learn to lean and depend on Him when you are feeling feeble.

Why is dishonesty discouraged in a Christian relationship?

Apply Bible principles from *Proverbs 4:24 ERV*

Don't bend the truth or say things that you know are not right.

A dishonest person is not obeying God's rules.

How can I protect my heart in a relationship?

Apply Bible principles from *Proverbs 4:23–27 NLT*

Guard your heart above all else, for it determines the course of your life. Avoid all perverse talk; stay away from corrupt speech. Look straight ahead, and fix your eyes on what lies before you. Mark out a straight path for your feet; stay on the safe path. Don't get sidetracked; keep your feet from following evil.

When Jesus sent the disciples out into Israel to preach and minister to the needs of the people, he instructed the disciples to be as wise as serpents yet harmless as doves. This is also excellent and suitable advice when entering into dating relationships.

Should I continue my friendships while I am in a relationship?

Apply Bible principles from *Proverbs 18:24 NIV*

There are "friends" who destroy each other, but a real friend sticks closer than a brother.

When you find a true friend, show your appreciation and gratitude because his or her loyalty can sometimes surpass that of family members. Remember, it is not important to have many friends; however, it is critical to have real ones.

Can a partner with the wrong motives destroy a relationship?

Apply Bible principles from *Proverbs 26:24-26 TLB*

A man with hate in his heart may sound pleasant enough, but don't believe him; for he is cursing you in his heart. Though he pretends to be so kind, his hatred will finally come to light for all to see.

In Christian relationships, remember our motives should be God's will, not our own.

Why is it smart to date an honorable person?

Apply Bible principles from *Proverbs 10:9 TNIV*

Whoever walks in integrity walks securely, but whoever takes crooked paths will be found out.

According to the Bible, honorable people exhibit conduct that is upright and pleasing to God. In Christian relationships, select a life partner who chooses a moral and decent lifestyle similar to your own. Bearing in mind, Christians are a witness for Christ at all times.

Are we defined by the contents of our heart?

Apply Bible principles from *Proverbs 27:19 ERV*

Just as you can see your own face reflected in water, so your heart reflects the kind of person you are.

Your partner's heart will reflect who he or she is as a person.

Can I trust a partner who gossips?

Apply Bible principles from *Proverbs 11:13 ERV*

People who tell secrets about others cannot be trusted. Those who can be trusted keep quiet.

Gossiping is a sin! It tears people down versus building them up. Any person displaying this behavior is not demonstrating Christian conduct and, therefore, cannot be trusted.

CHAPTER 25

Wisdom

W hen seeking knowledge in my personal life; I turn to my Bible. Why? Because I know that I will never encounter a "worldly" problem that biblical wisdom does not address. So, if you are searching for Christian solutions to resolve life's many predicaments, I encourage you to follow these three simple steps; (1) seek biblical wisdom, (2) study the Word of God, and (3) apply the principles of godly Scripture to your daily life. This chapter emphasizes the need for biblical wisdom in Christian dating relationships.

♥ ♥ ♥

Why is biblical wisdom invaluable in a dating relationship?

Apply Bible principles from *Proverbs 3:13 The Message*

You're blessed when you meet Lady Wisdom, when you make friends with Madame Insight. She's worth far more than money in the bank; her friendship is better than a big salary. Her value exceeds all the trappings of wealth; nothing you could wish for holds a candle to her. With one hand she gives long life, with the other she confers recognition. Her manner is beautiful, her life wonderfully complete. She's the very Tree of Life to those who embrace her. Hold her tight—and be blessed!

Biblical wisdom is priceless in any relationship, including work, church, friendships, and family associations.

Why shouldn't I compete with my partner in a Christian relationship?

Apply Bible principles from *Galatians 6:4 ERV*

Don't compare yourself with others. Just look at your own work to see if you have done anything to be proud of.

Christian relationships should be loving, caring, and supportive. Competition among partners will only lead to adversity.

While in a relationship, why must I keep God's Word close to me?

Apply Bible principles from *Hebrews 2:1 NLT*

...We must listen very carefully to the truth we have heard, or we may drift away from it.

Not only should we keep his word close, but we should apply the godly principles to our everyday life. Remember, there is much power in God's Word.

Why should I keep an open mind in a Christian relationship?

Apply Bible principles from *Proverbs 18:15 NLT*

Intelligent people are always open to new ideas. In fact, they look for them.

A closed mind is like a clenched fist; nothing gets out, but nothing gets in either.

How can my words uplift my partner?

Apply Bible principles of *Proverbs 16:24 ERV*

Kind words are like honey; they are easy to accept and good for your health.

Your kind and tenderhearted words should encourage each other.

Are there times when I should hold my tongue while communicating with my partner?

Apply Bible principles of *2 Timothy 2:23–24 ERV*

Stay away from foolish and stupid arguments. You know that these arguments grow into bigger arguments. As a servant of the Lord, you must not argue. You must be kind to everyone. You must be a good teacher, and you must be patient.

Christians must cultivate a disciplined tongue.

How should I handle a negative partner in a Christian relationship?

Apply Bible principles of *Psalms 37:1–4 NCV*

Don't be upset because of evil people. Don't be jealous of those who do wrong, because like the grass, they will soon dry up. Like green plants, they will soon die away. Trust the Lord and do good. Live in the land and feed on truth. Enjoy serving the Lord, and he will give you what you want.

In life, the more positive your responses are, the less negative your life will become. Remember, conflict cannot survive unless you participate.

Should I resist a partner who conceals resentment against me?

Apply Bible principles from *Job 5:2 NLT*

Surely resentment destroys the fool, and jealousy kills the simple.

Remember, hurting people tend to hurt other people. So, as Christians, try to be more compassionate and understanding of your partner. However, if this resentful pattern persists, the relationship is probably heading for trouble.

Why should I choose my relationship battles wisely with my partner?

Apply Bible principles from *Proverbs 19:11 TNIV*

A person's wisdom yields patience; it is to one's glory to overlook an offense.

Prioritize the issues. Discuss those which are substantive, and make a decision whether the smaller issues even need to be addressed.

♥　♥　♥

CHAPTER 26

Worry

When it comes to worrying, I have always thought of it this way, "You can either pray or worry—you should not have to do both!" Furthermore, they both consume the same amount of energy. This chapter emphasizes how ineffective worrying is when you have a Father, who will give you your heart's desire.

♥   ♥   ♥

How can I stop obsessing about finding a Christian mate?

Apply Bible principles from *Philippians 4:6–7 NLT*

Don't worry about anything; instead, pray about everything. Tell God what you need, and thank him for all he has done. Then you will experience God's peace, which exceeds anything we can understand. His peace will guard your hearts and minds as you live in Christ Jesus.

Worrying does not solve your problems; it creates more problems! God has a plan perfectly timed just for you.

Why is worrying considered a waste of time?

Apply Bible principles from *Matthew 6:27 ERV*

You cannot add any time to your life by worrying about it.

Instead of worrying, exercise your faith in the Lord! Worry is the greatest thief of joy.

How can I be supportive when my partner is consumed with worry?

Apply Bible principles from *Proverbs 12:25 NLT*

Worry weighs a person down; an encouraging word cheers a person up.

Show empathy and sympathy for those with a heavy heart.

How should I manage anxiety in a relationship?

Apply Bible principles from *1 Peter 5:7 TNIV*

Cast all your anxiety on him because he cares for you.

Anxiety can stem from excessive worry. Remember, you invest the same amount of energy to pray as you do to worry.

Where can I turn when my relationship concerns are stressing me out?

Apply Bible principles from *Matthew 11:28–30 ERV*

Come to me all of you who are tired from the heavy burden you have been forced to carry. I will give you rest. Accept my teaching. Learn from me. I am gentle and humble in spirit. And you will be able to get some rest. Yes, the teaching that I ask you to accept is easy. The load I give you to carry is light.

Our Heavenly Father is always there for us in times of despair. Remember, worrying does not rid you of your troubles instead it robs you of the strength needed to continue on your journey.

May Almighty God continue to bless you
and crown your efforts with success!

Printed in the United States
By Bookmasters